Mindful thoughts for
GARDENERS

First published in the UK in 2018 by

Leaping Hare Press

An imprint of The Quarto Group
The Old Brewery, 6 Blundell Street
London N7 9BH, United Kingdom
T (0)20 7700 6700 **F** (0)20 7700 8066
www.QuartoKnows.com

British Library Cataloguing-in-Publication Data
A catalogue record for this book is available from the British Library

ISBN: 978-1-78240-526-9

This book was conceived, designed and produced by

Leaping Hare Press

58 West Street, Brighton BN1 2RA, UK

Publisher: *Susan Kelly*
Creative Director: *Michael Whitehead*
Editorial Director: *Tom Kitch*
Art Director: *James Lawrence*
Commissioning Editor: *Monica Perdoni*
Project Editor: *Jenny Campbell*
Editor: *Jenni Davis*
Illustrator: *Lehel Kovacs*

Printed in China

3 5 7 9 10 8 6 4 2

Mindful thoughts for
GARDENERS

Sowing seeds of awareness

Clea Danaan

Leaping Hare Press

Contents

INTRODUCTION **The Message of the Garden**   6

Beginner's Mind   10

Seeds: Promises and Hopes   16

Soil: A Complex Relationship   22

Earthworms: The Underworld Alchemists   28

Roots: Real and Metaphorical   34

The Magic of Photosynthesis   40

The Duality of Weeds   46

Small Gardens   52

The Kingdom of Fungi   58

Recycling in the Garden   64

Plant Intelligence   70

Attitude of Gratitude   76

Going with the Flow   82

A Sense of Community   88

The Joy of Compost   94

The Scent of the Garden   100

Coping with Frustration   106

Listen to the Falling Rain   112

A Symbol of Hope   118

Bees: Essence of a Garden   124

No-dig Gardening   130

Permaculture   136

The Harvest   142

Cool-season Garden   148

The Garden Under Snow   154

ACKNOWLEDGEMENTS   160

The Message of
the Garden

There is something about a garden that's unlike any other environment. For many, the garden is a place to come home to oneself – with our hands tucked into living soil, we breathe in the scent of rosemary and mint, and we know who we are. The garden, whether a place for edibles or flowers or cactus, connects us to our physical self, our compassionate heart and our infinite soul. It is art, food and relationship with literally billions of beings. In the middle of this simple yet complex dance, we enter into mindful presence. We are here and now, this breath, this taste of fresh green leaf. Our hearts need green and growing things to feel strong and healthy, not just in terms of eating your greens, but in growing things green.

Certainly, it just feels good to be around plants. When you grow them yourself, you cultivate unique relationships directly with plants.

Keeping food local and fresh is a powerful act of presence and responsibility. Growing your own food is one of the best things you can do for yourself and for the planet. Grow a little extra and you spread the nourishment to others. Whether you keep a little pot of herbs in the kitchen or you grow a farm's worth, bringing mindfulness to your garden can extend the important work of gardening into the realm of spiritual practice and emotional health.

There is so much more to a garden than the plants themselves. A garden is nutrients and soil, bees and nematodes, water and light. When we begin to explore all the different parts of a garden, including ourselves, we see how vast and complex the garden truly is. We begin to see ourselves as a part of a greater whole. We see how our actions affect other parts of that whole, and how they in turn affect us. In this way, the garden is a tool for compassion and deeper understanding. It's a wisdom we come to by doing, though reading about the garden can guide us to a different sort of knowing, too. In these pages we will contemplate all aspects of the garden, including some of those inside the gardener. We will discover how the garden is inside us, too. For of course a garden is not just a garden.

This book is not a how-to guide, though perhaps you will get some new ideas as you read. Some of it may not apply to your specific garden, for you might grow more roses than I do, or you may live in a climate different from mine. But the message of the garden is the same everywhere. The plants, and the beings that support them, ask nothing of you but respect and care. They do not see your struggles and they do not judge. They invite you to be in relationship with them, separate but connected. Gardens reflect to us our essential nature, alive, seeking the light, hopeful for the future but unattached. Perhaps these thoughts do the same, inviting you to breathe, stretch and come back to your essential self.

Beginner's
Mind

Considering the mind of an infant exploring the garden anew can help us understand the Buddhist concept of beginner's mind – a mind that is open, without preconception. One summer day, when my daughter was about ten months old, I couldn't find her anywhere. Our house is fairly small, so a quick survey of rooms left me even more puzzled. The back door was open, but she couldn't walk yet, and had some trouble crawling off the raised deck. So I was surprised to discover her all the way up the garden (a long way to crawl), her chubby, cloth-nappied bottom settled happily in front of the tomato jungle. Later I saw how she got herself to the garden, crawling on hands and feet, lifting her tender knees up to protect them from the scratchy grass and wood chips. This was one determined baby.

Once she got herself up the garden, she sought out green globes of immature tomatoes, picked one, took a bite, made a face while tossing it aside and moved on to another. I added many one-bite green tomatoes to my compost that year. It sort of annoyed me, but at the same time I celebrated her determination and curiosity. I found it fascinating that she knew how to get her little self to the garden, and knew that in theory those tomatoes were edible, but then didn't revise her strategy when they tasted bitter and green. Or perhaps she didn't set out with 'eating tomatoes' as a goal, but rather just met each opportunity on the path as it arose.

My daughter had approached the garden with some sort of goal or idea in mind, but also an open mind, a beginner's mind. Each tomato was a new opportunity, a new choice point. Whereas I came to the garden with an agenda, she just found herself before a green tangle of plants and chose to take a bite.

KEEPING AN OPEN MIND

To be successful as gardeners we need our list of things to do, and we are constantly reading blog posts and books or taking classes to learn more. I just learned, for instance, that I have to pinch off the first generation of pepper flowers in order to get larger peppers. Now I've added that task to my to-do list, I get better peppers. (I always wondered why they were so tiny!)

When considering a mindful approach to gardening, however, we also need to gently hold the idea of beginner's mind. Yes, we have our plans and agenda, but each garden, each pepper plant, each flower, is new. It has never existed before. Nor has this moment in time.

We are beginners in this moment. When we approach a plant or a task with an open mind, we enter 'original mind', the place that mindfulness can bring us that is hard to express through words. We exist and the pepper plant exists now, here. In beginner's mind, we release ourselves from the need to achieve anything. We can chomp a green tomato just because it's there.

LIMITED AND LIMITLESS

Here is the challenge: can we hold the dialectic – both/and – of plans and open mind? Limitations are important, healthy parts of our world. Yet we can get trapped in our limitations, not seeing the garden for the pepper flowers. Our mind becomes demanding, and we get stuck in striving. Beginner's mind helps us step out of these limitations, this striving, and become boundless. We are simultaneously limited and limitless.

My baby daughter did have an agenda, whether she was aware of it or not: to learn. The human mind has a pull to grow, reach, understand. These are important parts of who we are, throughout all stages of life. This striving to expand our relationship with the world should not, however, be nurtured at the expense of the calm, centred awareness that keeps us connected to our core self, which no striving can change. We can be the tomato plant, reaching into the soil for nutrients and up to the sun for light, yet inhabiting its tomato self only in the here and now. In this way, our mind is open and ready, containing both our limitations and our boundlessness.

Seeds:
Promises and Hopes

A seed is the epitome of hope. Inside a seed rests 'life concentrate'. Everything a plant needs to reach first down into the darkness and then upwards towards the light is held safe in the hard containment of the seed coat. Inside the suitcase of the seed coat waits a tiny future root, a tiny future shoot and all the food the seedling will need to get started. Also inside the little package of life are invisible instructions telling the seed just what it's here to do.

As gardeners, we use seeds as prayers, little promises of what is to come. We humans eat seeds daily: rice, wheat, sunflower, pea, bean, peanut, sesame . . . Some seeds are harder to digest than others, as a seed wants to be not consumed but continued, carried on. Some of us can't digest certain seeds at all; my body reads gluten as a toxin, so I don't eat wheat, rye or barley seeds in any form. Perhaps the surge of allergies to various seeds is the planet's way of urging us to respect seeds: stop taking them for granted; stop dousing them with poisons; stop modifying them – respect.

WHAT SEEDS ARE NEAR YOU AT THIS MOMENT?

Seeds are all around us. Outside my office window hangs a bird feeder filled with black sunflower seeds. The chickadees and house finches who visit the feeder each day certainly respect seeds. Watching the black-capped chickadees feed is a meditation in life. A feathery tuxedoed gentleman bird lands on the wire over my patio, chirping about his surroundings. He swoops down to the lip of the feeder, looks about once, then dips into the cage of seeds and chooses just one. He flits back up to the box elder tree, removes the hard seed coat with his beak and eats the fatty rich seed in a few mincing bites. He scrapes his beak side to side on a branch, cheeps a few times to his companions – they often come in twos and threes – and swoops down for another seed.

From where I sit, even in the middle of winter, I can see this feeder filled with seeds, but it is not the only seed close to me at this moment. On the shelf to my left I see a bag of sunflower seeds for the feeder. Above me waits a miniature pumpkin I've saved, a vault of seeds I will plant in the spring. On the little deck outside I can see a few linden seeds that found their way here on the wind last autumn. I can see a few dried rosehips on the brown and dormant wild rose bushes in the garden. Not far from where I sit, in my kitchen cupboard, I can find all manner of seeds in the forms of grains, flours, nut butters and the like. They are all around us because seeds are life; seeds are nourishment; seeds are promises and hopes and the future. Look around you, what seeds are nearby at this moment?

NOT JUST A METAPHOR

For a gardener who starts at least some plants from seeds, a pile of seeds invokes a giddy excitement. At a community seed swap, I cannot wipe the happy grin off my face as I dig through my friends' offerings. When the first display of garden seed packets appears at the natural food store in spring, I send out a whoop of joy and don't really care what other shoppers think. Few things make me happier. Seeds mean spring and the garden. For people on this planet who can't just mosey into a natural food store or a garden nursery to casually buy a few paper packets of this and that, seeds hold even more importance. To the farmer in Malawi or rural India, seeds mean they and their children will live another year. For them, the seed is not just a metaphor.

And really, the same is true for us all. In developed nations, we can forget that our lives depend on seeds. This is why seed banks around the world store a variety of rare and common seeds, keeping them safe for the benefit of humanity as well as the plants. In 2015, Syrian agricultural researchers made the first withdrawal of seeds from the Svalbard Global Seed Vault – sometimes referred to as 'the doomsday vault' – since its creation in 2008. The seeds were planted in Morocco and Lebanon, after the drought-resistant varieties of wheat were destroyed by the conflict in Syria. We are all united by our reliance on plants and their seeds. By growing, protecting and saving seeds yourself, you are a part of this web that reaches across all cultural barriers. The seeds that keep us alive depend on us to do the same for them.

Soil:
A Complex Relationship

Though we call it 'dirt', and refer to something impure as 'soiled', we depend on the complex matrix that is soil for our lives. Plants can be grown in controlled conditions in water, but most of the food we eat, and virtually all of the oxygen-producing land plants, grow in soil. Black, humusy soil; thick red clay; dusty light-brown silt – soil varies immensely, depending on where you are and how it was formed. You can smell some of its history simply by scooping up a handful of earth. Metals and rocks smell tangy and dusty, while the sweet smell of organic matter comes from certain kinds of bacteria. Bits of decaying organic matter like shredded leaves smell like the wet and mossy forest floor. Threads of fungus give off a mushroomy smell. Soil that has sat untouched and too wet can give off an unpleasant decaying smell, which comes from the lack of oxygen. What does the scent of your own garden soil tell you about your land and climate? What images or associations spring to mind when you take a deep whiff of your soil?

As gardeners, we can deepen our understanding of the process of gardening by looking into the network of relationships that makes up the soil. It isn't just dirt, but a fluctuating dance of microbes, bugs, minerals, plants and even ourselves. Understanding and cultivating this relationship consciously, we enter into our own rich darkness. Touch, smell and maybe even taste the soil, and your body sinks a little deeper into the groundedness of the garden. We sense more deeply the complexity of life, the dynamism of soil and gut and decay that all lead to growth and life.

Not just the yin and the yang, but the swirl and flow between these poles, the strands of the web of relationship that is a garden.

NOURISHING THE DANCE OF LIFE

When we nestle a tiny seed into the soil, we plant a prayer. We ask the soil to protect and nourish this seed of life. Then we wave our magic wand – the kind that water comes out of – and whisper a spell that sets off a series of relationships that will eventually lead to a salad or a soup gracing our table. We pray: *grow*. The soil wraps its damp darkness around this little seed, this promise, and when the seed bursts its skin and reaches out with a tiny root filament, the soil says yes. The roots grasp on to tiny particles of sand and stone, and the soil hugs back. It affirms the life of the sprout, holding it in place and time. It gently feeds it nutrients and water in just the right amount. Slowly the sprout turns into a seedling, then a plant, eventually producing a fruit. All of this growth is supported by the soil tucked around its roots.

We nourish the dance of life when we build garden soil. Adding compost, manure, minerals and other amendments feeds the network of bacteria, fungi, nematodes and earthworms. Eventually, this care will resonate into macro communities as the soil feeds plants and the plants feed animals, including us humans.

The nourished soil, together with the ancient minerals present since before life began on Earth, feeds that seed you planted. It holds and nourishes it like a mother holding her child. As the child of the Earth, the plant grows bigger and stronger, it reaches deep down inside this support network. Only with strong support is it able to also stand tall and reach into the sky, like a dancer, strong and lithe. Eventually, the plant is ready to gift itself to the flow of life.

When you pull a carrot from the soil, dust off the earth and hand it to your neighbour, you are participating in the vast strands of life that begin in the soil.

Perhaps we, too, feel a similar support when we participate in this dance. The soil holds us. It literally holds our weight. It nourishes our food, which in turn nourishes our bodies. It accepts what we give it, and gives us back the gift of green and growing things. Because of the complex darkness of living soil, we have shade from the oak, the sweetness of strawberries and even each breath of fresh air. And when our journey is complete, the cells that make up our bodies will return to the soil, eventually gifting our nourishment to the cycle of life.

Earthworms:
The Underworld Alchemists

A soil's health derives from its ability to embrace and transform death. The decomposition rate of soil – the transformation of fallen leaves and dead bugs into more soil – determines soil health, or its ability to support more life. It's hard for us to see this actually happening, for it does so microscopically and at a slower pace than we humans like to do things. But as much as soil is a thing, it is a process, constantly changing. One of the key players in the game of soil is the earthworm, slowly pushing its way through the damp darkness to churn organic matter into soil.

Have you ever placed a worm back on a garden bed after rudely plucking it from the soil and watched how it searches about and then returns back from whence it came? I wonder what it is looking for precisely as it winds this way and that, choosing just the right spot to re-enter the earth. Not an opening, for it seems to just be absorbed by the soil through its own accordion action. A softer bit? A tasty bit? When it finds what it's looking for, it doesn't really use much muscle to move what seems to me to be very dense soil. It doesn't seem to push its way into the soil the way I might push through a crowd. It just sort of becomes the soil. And yet I do not see it eating, not in the way I have watched a wasp scrape at wood or a caterpillar chomp a leaf. It is quite literally one with soil. It *rebecomes* one with the soil when it returns from our light and airy world to the dense dark of earth and stone. The worm can teach us about being one with our own surroundings, as we breathe the air, press our feet into the soil and soak sun into our skin.

THE EARTH TRANSFORMED

Atop the soil, we can see what the worm leaves behind, called castings. The worm is a piece of intestine without a greater body cavity, and it churns the soil through its intestine body and pushes it out its back end. In some ways the earth itself is the worm's body, as well as the thing it consumes. The worm is the earth transforming itself. Somehow in the magic of this process, the soil that comes out of a worm is transformed: it contains fewer toxins and more available nutrients than earth that has not been 'wormed'.

Sometimes earthworms are too effective. In some forests where invasive worm species have moved in, usually because humans bring them there (as when a fisherman disposes of his unused bait at the side of a lake), the worms eat up more of the leaf litter than is good for that forest ecosystem. The trees' roots end up exposed, tree seedlings get eaten by deer and there is less nutrient matter to slowly sink into the soil. Worm casting provide good, quick nutrients; in our garden, these feed fast-growing annuals like petunias and cabbage. In a slower growing forest, however, nutrients need to break down and release slowly, over a much longer stretch of time, thus the importance of leaf litter.

CONTEMPLATION ON A WORM

So an earthworm is a meditation on transformation, but also on how transformation needs to happen in its own just-right time. We can learn from the worm about taking in the world around us and transmuting it into nourishment and wisdom we can use for more growth. We can learn, too, that sometimes that process of change needs to go more slowly than we would like. To transform toxins, we need time. We need the support of the world around us just as the worm needs the weight of the land. We need the good stuff to be greater than the toxic bits. And then, in time, we can release what we no longer need. We can move forward, and we can share what we've gained with the world, perhaps helping to serve life in ever-widening circles around us.

In contemplating worms, I'm reminded of the childhood song, 'The worms crawl in, the worms crawl out, the worms play pinochle on your snout!' Worms, and their lesser known companions the nematodes and other microorganisms, are the underworld alchemists. They take what could not support life force anymore and turn it into a gift for the living. In supporting worms in our wormeries and beds, we too take on the role of the alchemist. With compost and water, we nurture the process of transformation. The gold we end up with comes in the form of carrots and marigolds, and the cycle continues to unfold.

Roots:
Real and Metaphorical

As gardeners, we are always putting down roots. The plants we partner with stretch their own roots deep into the soil in search of nourishment and water. In tending the plants, we also put down roots energetically wherever we garden. People who relocate to new houses often feel more grounded to a place by planting even a few herbs in a pot on the patio or windowsill. Farmers, of course, root their families so deeply to place that it becomes a part of who they are. The longer the lifespan of the plant, the greater the sense of connection and commitment to the land. By planting asparagus, fruit trees or roses, for example, you sign up for a long-term relationship with the land. As you tend the soil, the land supports you. If your garden contains edibles, you literally become a part of the land as you consume the gifts of the earth. This connection through gardens is true of communities as well as individuals. When neighbours create a community garden, they create common ground. We all ground through putting down roots.

A NUTRITIONAL POWERHOUSE

Roots are a plant's primary way of gaining nourishment. Tiny hairs on the root reach out into the soil, using ion exchange to absorb nutrients. A plant that has been in the soil a long time has grown a great beard of hairy root filaments, not unlike the connections we form as members of a community. All those filaments and folds help connect a plant not only to nutrients in the soil, but also to other organisms around the plant. Through fungi in the soil, plants' roots of the same and different species can exchange nutrients and chemicals. When you pull up a root, many of these finer threads break off and remain in the soil to decay, adding organic matter.

In soils where nutrients are scarce, the roots' length can far exceed the height of the plant. These root structures help build the soil as well as the plant.

Roots not only suck up nutrients, they also act as the plant's root cellar. In winter, plants store sugars, starches and nutrients in their roots while the rest of the plant goes dormant. For us gardeners, this translates as improved taste and nutrition in root vegetables, such as carrots and potatoes, that have been left in the soil through a frost or two. We crave root stews in autumn and winter because roots store well, but also because consuming a plant's roots gives us Earth medicine at a time when we seek the grounded stillness of winter. In traditional Chinese medicine, root vegetables are balanced and nourishing, neither too cleansing nor too rich. Many root vegetables are said to clear toxins, cleanse the blood and support digestion.

The following meditation explores your own energetic roots. You may want to keep in mind the above thoughts as you feel your own roots and sense deep into the Earth.

ROOT MEDITATION

Sit in a place where you will not be disturbed. Outside is best, but not necessary. Sitting with your back against a tree or near a favourite plant would be a perfect place to practise this meditation on your own roots, but sitting on the floor indoors or even on a chair is fine.

Close your eyes and feel your sitting bones press into the ground. Notice how the ground presses back against you. Now reach your awareness past this connection, sensing into the space below you. Reach your awareness down until you enter the soil beneath you. Feel any change in your body as you connect your energy into the Earth.

In your mind's eye, see the image of the Tree of Life, a tree with branches reaching upwards balanced by roots reaching down. Impose this image over yourself until you become the Tree of Life. Your body is the trunk, your energetic branches reach into the energy space around and above your head, and the energy you reach downward into the Earth is your roots. Breathe for a few moments as a great tree, connecting Earth with body with sky. Breath and trust whatever feelings arise. You are rooted to the Earth.

What do your roots feel as they reach into the soil? Does it feel good to be rooted, or do you feel stuck in one place? Can you gently open your energetic roots to the nourishment of the Earth? Allow yourself to connect deeply to the ground beneath you.

When you are finished, pull your energy back into your body but stay connected by a few strands with the Earth to keep you grounded. Breathe and come into your normal senses.

The Magic of
Photosynthesis

Inside all the beautiful green leaves of the plant kingdom, magic occurs. Some call it science, but really it is both. Photons of light bounce off chlorophyll molecules, setting off a chain of events that produces plant energy in the form of glucose, and the by-product of oxygen. Because of this 'technology' created by plants 450 million years ago, we are alive today. We grow photosynthesis factories in our gardens. Whether you regard the process as purely scientific or a miracle, or both, you tuck little seeds into soil as an invocation of photosynthesis. A garden or a farm is a request of the universe to please transform sunlight, carbon dioxide and water into energy that we can use to dance and dream and love. Most of the time, this request is honoured, and we get both fresh air and salad in the process. Miraculous!

Plants photosynthesize without thinking about it. They don't have to try to make sugar, they just do. Perhaps we can learn from them in this – be grateful for the natural processes our bodies carry out without conscious effort, and express our gifts just as 'something we do'. Sometimes our gifts feel easy to execute, and we feel nourished by them. At other times, they feel more like a chore, or expressing our gifts pushes against self-doubt or fear. We can remember the plants photosynthesizing for the good of all, and settle into our own gifts without fear.

A MATTER OF BALANCE

Photosynthesis is a balance of give and take, which is something I am learning to do myself. I'm a giver, having taken on the role early in life to care for everyone around me; but givers can easily slip into over-giving without even realizing until they are exhausted, cranky and have a headache. Plants have no choice in the matter; if there is not enough light, enough water or enough carbon, they cannot produce glucose and oxygen. There has to be a balance. Of course, the same is true for human giving and receiving, but the breakdown occurs more slowly than in a plant. Humans who give and give eventually fall apart and can give no more. Their bodies demand care and attention. Is there a way we can learn from plants and other natural systems of balance to take care of ourselves now, before we crash? One way we can nourish ourselves is by eating plants, literally taking the products of photosynthesis into our own bodies. One of the quickest ways to balance and health is to eat lots and lots of plants.

We are not plants, but perhaps we can gain more balance in our own giving and receiving by being more like a plant for a moment. Sitting still, breathing, being in this moment only. In other words, practising mindfulness. When we are mindful, we allow ourselves to settle into observation of what is, ebb and flow. It is then that we more readily notice in what ways we have 'efforted' ourselves out of balance, and we can gently see how to right ourselves. By gently witnessing our resistance to what is, we can begin either to dissolve that resistance or to take calm steps towards changes that need to be made. We seek to return to the balance that a healthy plant naturally expresses.

EXPRESSING OUR LIGHT

Photosynthesis is respiration in reverse. Respiration is essentially breathing, and it means to re-spirit, to re-breathe. We breathe, and we are filled with spirit again and again. Whether we breathe mindfully as we sit still as a rooted plant, or we re-spirit as we garden in a moving meditation, we reflect the natural processes of energy production and transformation of light. In spiritual teachings across cultures, we are also made of light, the bright light that glows within. Expressing our gifts – in a balanced dance of give and take – is a way we share this light with the world. 'Synthesis' means to put together, so we perform our own version of photosynthesis – putting together light – when we take the experiences we have had, our natural gifts and the skills we have developed, synthesize them and share them with the world.

The Duality of
Weeds

We gardeners consider the 'worst' weeds to be those we just can't get rid of. Bindweed and 'tree of heaven' are the worst offenders in my garden; they have multiple ways to spread and will grow just about anywhere. No matter how many I pull up, there are always more. While I cannot guarantee that my vegetable garden will do well this year, or that my flowers will continue to thrive, I can utterly and completely guarantee that these weeds, as well as many others, will be a part of my garden this summer.

Is there much else in life we can rely on so thoroughly? I suppose it's a matter of supply and demand. We don't invest in weeds, for we know they will be there. We invest in stocks, for the risk makes them valuable. Why do we so devalue something we can depend on? Instead of devaluing them, I have learned to determine weeds' purposes, for it is a relationship I can depend on.

THE USEFULNESS OF WEEDS

The kinds of weeds present in a garden or other habitat can tell us about the land itself, as well as what minerals may be present or lacking. Foxtail, horsetail and willow indicate that the land will be wet and swampy, during at least part of the year. Chicory and bindweed indicate compacted soil. Dandelions, mullein, yarrow and nettles indicate an acidic soil, while field pepperwort and campion show you the soil is alkaline. Gardeners can use these indicators to tell us either what will grow well in this soil, or what remediation is needed.

One reason these weeds grow in their particular soil conditions is that they can, but another reason is that they offer some remediation to the soil's challenges.

Bindweed and clover work to break up soil. Dandelions and sunflowers accumulate minerals in their plant tissue, which can either help pull minerals from deep down and make them available to surface-growing plants, or actually remove excess minerals from the soil. This is so effective it is used to remediate toxic soil. Here we again see an example of the dynamic relationship between soil and plants. We are reminded that plants aren't just growing things, but have a purpose in a web we only slightly understand.

We can benefit from these weeds' gifts directly as well. Dandelions, when one eats the whole of the plant, provide a complete protein. They are highly nutritious and, since they are so easy to grow, could help to provide a solution to malnutrition in some parts of the world. One of my favourite weeds to eat is nettle, which also happens to be one of the most nutritious plants on Earth. Learning how to eat the weeds in your garden cultivates a whole new relationship with the land.

A MINDFUL APPROACH

Transforming our understanding of weeds, however, is only half of a mindful relationship with these plants. The other way we need to relate to them from a mindful perspective is to notice our resistance to them. A mindful approach to weeds does not try to make a bad situation good, although there is nothing inherently wrong with doing so. A mindful approach simply sits with the weeds as they are, without trying to manipulate their existence into something that benefits us. Notice how when I say 'weed', the feeling in your body is different from when I say 'pea plant' or 'peony'. Neither response is good or bad, it's just an opportunity to notice how we cling to one thing or another. We become attached to something as 'good' or 'bad'. That attachment itself is also neither good nor bad, it just is. It is an opportunity to notice, and then to notice what arises once we develop awareness.

When I allow bindweed to simply be a part of my garden, I don't have to surrender to it. I still pull up as much as I can, stuff it into a black plastic bag and stick the bag in my hot driveway to cook the seeds before adding the mass to the compost. But no longer do I fight the bindweed. No longer do I curse and stress about how my garden is less than perfect and I am a failure as a gardener because of its presence. I just accept that part of my garden is bindweed, and move forward from the place of acceptance.

Small
Gardens

Sometimes we have to accept that we don't have
the time or the space for a large garden. Rather
than regard this as a failure or a deficiency,
we can approach it as an opportunity
to get creative. Gardens are about
relationships – with plants, the Earth,
our communities and ourselves. Any
garden is a gift and a journey, even
if it is one little pot of marigolds.
The garden is what we make of it. The
popularity of fairy gardens illustrates
how a small garden can be just as
rewarding and fun as a big plot of land.

In fact, I would argue that an apartment needs a garden even more than a house. I've lived in apartments twice, and plants made all the difference. In the first, I was home for the summer from college, and my mother and I put tomatoes and flowers on the balcony, which overlooked a busy street. Across this busy street, a family was evicted while we lived there, all their stuff dumped on the lawn. We knew drug deals were likely happening all around us, though we weren't in any immediate danger. The pots of plants sitting proudly on the artificial grass-covered balcony brought a sense of normalcy and nature to our space.

In the second apartment I lived in, we didn't have a balcony. My boyfriend and I and our two cats shared our space with a lot of indoor potted plants. The cats especially enjoyed them. I learned which plants they liked to eat and which they ignored. As soon as we relocated to a house with a garden, they stopped gnawing on potted plants. I knew just how they felt. I think without the plants we had, though, cleansing the air and bringing us green leaves and dark soil, I would have become rather depressed in our apartment. Small spaces need plants. Plant people, and cats, need plants.

MAKING THE MOST OF A SMALL SPACE

If you live in a small space with only a balcony or a patio, there is so much you can do to create a tiny farm of your own. In many ways, pots are easier to work with than a full-sized garden. While I have a large suburban plot, I always grow a few things in pots myself. Pots are portable, so I can move them in and out of microclimates, or get them inside for a hailstorm or a frost as needed. They are easy to water. For me, a primary benefit of potted plants is that I am not struggling with the heavy clay soil in my garden. And again, there are those cute fairy gardens. Pots can be filled with pretty rocks and shells, or even tiny wind chimes, to make them not only potted gardens, but little spaces of retreat and magic.

What do you want to grow? Potted gardens, such as herbs in the kitchen, tropical plants in the sunroom or tomatoes on your balcony, offer the flexibility that our modern culture so often requires. A portable potted garden allows us to connect with soil and plants without a great deal of space. A potted garden allows you to control temperature and water. Therefore, you can use the potted garden to express your unique gardening dreams. Do you miss your home climate, or do you wish you lived someplace different? Perhaps you can grow a plant from that region in a sunny spot or even a terrarium. Just as you might wear a dress from a culture you feel connected to, a small garden can offer you a bit of the energy of your dreams and inner self.

Living in a small space doesn't just limit you to pots and hanging gardens, however. Consider other possibilities for spending time in the garden, such as community gardens, nearby gardens and school gardens. Volunteering at a local school garden, or tending an elderly neighbour's garden, is an opportunity for service and getting in time with those good soil microbes and green brothers and sisters. Every plant, every plot of tended soil, makes the world a greener, fresher and more caring place. Every moment spent in a garden fills your heart with the compassion of green and growing things.

The Kingdom of
Fungi

Throughout the soil, snaking their way through rotting
logs, are the hidden wizards of the natural world.
Mycelium, the lacing white strands produced by some
species of fungi, transform organic matter into rich,
nourishing humus. Gardeners are beginning to learn
what forests have known for millennia – that rich soil
comes largely from the work of fungi – and are learning
to invite them into the garden instead of trying
to destroy them. While it is true that some
fungi are responsible for plant diseases like
rusts, mildews and tree fungus, most fungi
in the garden are beneficial. Mushrooms
and mycelium cycle carbon, taking it

out of plant matter and into the soil. They create soil by breaking down wood and other fibres into fluffy dark humus. Certain fungi even help protect plants from consumption by insects and herbivores.

TUNING IN TO FUNGI

Mycelium grows from some types of fungi, and these inconspicuous tendrils do more than just break down plant matter. They also form part of nature's Internet. By connecting into the network of mycelium, plant roots are actually able to communicate via chemical signals to other plants. This communication network covers large distances and can link different species together. The network helps plants share nutrients and builds their immune systems by helping to fight off pathogens. In our information age, we could potentially learn a lot from the fungi, who perfected the information highway long ago.

The mindful gardener knows to sit and listen, to learn from this kingdom of fungi, mushrooms and mycelium. What do the travelling strands of white tell us about cycles of life? One thing I have learned from fungi is that they are not all the same, and the different types have different functions. Some break down plant lignin while others transform cellulose. Another kind of fungi just recently discovered, called endophytic fungi, live in between plant cells and protect plants from herbivores and drought. The world of fungi is vast and varied, and we are beginners in understanding it. This sings to me of the value of diversity. I am reminded to listen to the varied voices of others, especially those different from me and what I am used to.

MASTERS OF MINDFULNESS

Fungi reminds us, too, that change, healing and growth all take time. With our relatively short lifespans and our tendency to separate ourselves from nature, we humans want things to happen immediately. I want it to be time to plant seeds now, even though it is still late winter. Then I want the plants to grow, bloom and fruit. As they grow hidden from our eyes in mysterious processes, the slow-growing bodies of fungi – perhaps more than other beings in the garden – remind us that we need to allow time for ourselves to grow and evolve. Sometimes we have to let things sit awhile as the threads of transformation do their work.

Curiously, when we become present to the moment, mindful of existing right now, we step gently out of our impatience and hurry. Perhaps mushrooms are masters of mindfulness. Certainly they are not wrapped up in their minds, stressing about what particle of cellulose to deconstruct next. Fungi, and plants too, can become teachers, showing us how to be present to what is, and to allow changes to happen in the natural flow of time.

Fungi teach us about balance, about interconnection and about the strength of diversity. They strengthen the garden and the forest, and they may prove to be one of the keys to a sustainable future. Researchers are very interested in fungi's potential in the field of medicine, especially in regards to cancer care. Certain fungi are able to remediate toxically polluted sites. A team of designers have created ways to grow leather and wood substitutes out of mushrooms, which costs less and is more sustainable than cattle farming or cutting down trees for lumber. Everywhere they grow, fungi produce rich soil, a gift to gardeners. Next time you see them coming up in your garden, send them thanks, for they are likely creating health in the soil.

Recycling
in the Garden

I'm always so excited and proud of myself when I
forage in my garden and garage and discover just the
board I need for a new raised bed, or I dig up and haul
enough rocks from the back garden to the front to
cobble together a little wall. Repurposing is ecological –
reuse reduces waste – and economic. It feels creative
and resourceful, like throwing together a meal from
the last of the leftover ingredients. Also, I love instant
gratification. When I get the idea for a project, I want
to execute it now, not after three trips to the hardware
store, so I'm thrilled to find materials on-site and
repurpose them. The same is true for plants, as when
we turn them into compost, it is a form of recycling.

Gardens lend themselves to repurposing and reusing. Whether it's a plant from a neighbour, a gate of wooden pallets or a chicken coop of scrap wood, recycling turns the garden into an ever-evolving masterpiece of innovation. As you spend more time in a garden, you get to know it better, from the way light hits different areas throughout the changing seasons to where certain soils can be found. Friends and resources show up, then move on to greener pastures. One year you decide to plant a pear tree, another time you contemplate adding chickens. Children come and go, and the pear tree gets bigger. The garden is a long conversation between the land and the gardener.

MEMORIES OF RECYCLING

Life is made up of stories. One thing I love about using repurposed objects in the garden is the stories behind them. My chicken coop is an example: the wood was given to me by a friend who found a pile of wood scraps in her basement. That same friend later organized a local food feast and invited me to contribute using my chickens' eggs. Though she and I don't see each other often, I think of her frequently, my henhouse a reminder of our cherished connection. Throughout my garden are other connections, other stories: the bricks for our firepit from a friend's crumbled shed; raised beds formed of discarded benches; a swing made from an old tyre; raspberry plants from a friend's garden. And while it may sound like my garden is a regular scrapyard, it is the opposite. From scraps and labour, I've crafted a garden oasis. I've learned from the garden and life to reuse and make the world a more beautiful place.

Over time, the garden grows and so do we. Recycling in the garden is a metaphor for life. As we grow, we are able to see in new light what we once set aside. Past events can nourish you now, giving you strength. You grow a little taller, a little stronger and live to tell the tale. What truly no longer serves you, toss into the universal compost, where Life will churn your experiences into nourishment for others. That's recycling in action.

THE ULTIMATE IN RECYCLING

Augustus Jenkins Farmer, author of *Deep-Rooted Wisdom: Skills and Stories from Generations of Gardeners*, takes repurposing a step further. For his garden structures, he grows his own materials using vines and bamboo. Growing your own not only creates whimsical and unique garden shapes, it vastly reduces the carbon footprint of one's garden. Most trellises bought at a garden centre are, he says, made 'overseas with "downcycled" materials, and shipped using packing supplies and gas. Why contribute to the pollution and waste?' Structures made from recycled wood, plastic or metal are simply kept out of the landfill for a while, whereas his naturally grown structures are not produced with any chemicals and will only end up on the compost heap. They stay completely out of the industrial cycle, and he gets to spend more time in his garden instead of shopping for materials.

Recycling, repurposing and reusing can come in many forms. Diversity yields strength. The garden can be a place of stories, our own and others. It is

a network of relationships: between ourselves and
the world, between the garden and ourselves, within
the garden itself and even within ourselves. In this
way, the garden becomes a process. We evolve together,
bringing our unique strengths to the table of life,
having fun as we do so.

Plant
Intelligence

We humans are just beginning to redefine intelligence
and emotion. For so long we have made the idea of
intelligence fit into a narrow definition of being able
to score well on certain tests. This understanding has
blinded us against the different forms of intelligence
in our own species as well as in others, including in
plants. Today, many studies exist on plant intelligence,
but I suspect they are still regarded with a certain
humour and scepticism. Yet intelligence means the
ability to take information from various sources,
synthesize that information and react in a way that
demonstrates understanding. Plants are extremely
adept at this process.

Consider the wisdom in your garden. Hundreds of plants communicating with each other and responding to the conditions around them. They send out signals via fungi and root chemicals in the soil, essentially speaking to other plants for quite a distance around them. Through their leaves they send out other messages, such as when your grass tells birds it is being consumed, asking for help against insect invaders. Science fiction story or woo-woo wishful thinking? No – just the smell your grass emits when it is cut by the mower. The scent is a cry for help.

OUR ROLE IN THE GARDEN

How can we gardeners tap into this intelligence? In all honesty, as I contemplated this question, my first thought was to wonder if plants try to communicate directly with us. I did exactly what humans have done for thousands of years, focusing on myself as the important part of the relationship with plants. This bias, while innocent and understandable, underlies our current climate crisis. It can lead us gardeners to miss a lot of valuable information. When I abandon my perspective as the centre of the garden, and instead shift it to one part of the whole, my understanding changes.

What is our role in the garden? When I step out of the role of benevolent ruler or artist sculpting the land, when I become part of the garden itself, what do I become? I am the one with hands, tools and motility. I have a perspective of 'my' land that includes perspectives the plants cannot have, such as property boundaries, overhead electrical wires and council by-laws. I know what vegetables my children like to eat. I stress about water bills. For me, these thoughts are a part of my garden. To the plants, not so much. These are the thoughts of a creative ruler. What about the plants' ideas?

A PLANT'S PERSPECTIVE

First, I have to look beyond the plant as something that serves me, and try to imagine its own perspective. A bean plant is a means to an end when I am Manager of the garden. From its own perspective, however, a bean plant is itself, growing near other plants of its type. It has formed agreements with several fungi in the soil to transform available nitrogen into a more plant-available resource. The beans it produces are a hope to carry on its life force in future plants. While we could argue about whether or not a plant considers itself a 'self', it does relate to plants, animals and fungi around it as a distinct entity.

I can take this information and use it to my advantage as one who wants to eat beans, providing the bean plant with the right fungi for optimum nutrient absorption, but I can also use this as an opportunity to simply expand my perspective of what a garden actually is. I am a part of a vast network of plants, some of which would grow just fine without me, while others are only growing in this plot of earth because I put them there and keep them watered. I then consider other networks I am a part of that also include perspectives different from mine. My Mexican neighbours, whose days share similarities with mine but whose lives are different in ways I cannot imagine. My Amerindian neighbour, who is also a veteran. The man across the street who was born in Vietnam but was adopted and grew up here. I see them regularly, and we share certain values and hopes, but our lives are different in other ways. We are a garden. Our intelligences overlap, and they differ.

When I consider the intelligence of my garden, or the perspectives of my neighbours, I am filled with respect. I am curious and open. I feel gratitude.

Attitude of
Gratitude

A good way to stop anxiety in its tracks is to feel gratitude. Feeling a sense of thankfulness and even wonder for our lives is a form of mindfulness, which is why this works to halt anxiety. Even severe anxiety, as in a panic attack, lessens its grip a little when we sit mindfully with what is happening right now. I am alive. I am feeling sensations that I don't like, but I am feeling.

I need to remember this when I'm feeling cranky about my garden. Either something has died, or it's not yet time to plant, or I have only one measly grape on the vine. One grape, not one cluster. Yes, really. While I can allow myself to feel frustration and disappointment, I can also shift my perspective just a little to include gratitude. That one grape is really very pretty, and this grape vine is still alive. I have soil in which to plant a grape vine. I have a garden in which to cultivate that soil. Then my single grape becomes a celebration, instead of a whine fest.

PLANTS AS THERAPY

Gardens have pulled me out of some very dark times. After I moved to Colorado with my future husband, we lived in an apartment for six months. During that time, his father died and I flailed about trying to figure out what I wanted to do with my life. When we moved to a house with a garden, I still didn't know what to do with myself, but I sunk my hands into the soil and felt a sense of myself again. That garden was a ray of light in a confusing time of life. Years later, when my own father died, I bought my mother some pansies, herbs and tomatoes and put them in pots outside her home. The garden had been Dad's realm, and I felt his presence strongly as I tucked soil around the roots of the new plants. I returned home after his service to find my grape vine (same one!) had come into leaf in my absence. Later I will tell you about my pear trees that gave me hope in this midst of a health crisis. I feel such gratitude for that first Colorado garden, those potted plants at my mother's house, the grape vine and the pear trees. Green and growing things have long centred me and offered me gifts of life.

Gardening lends itself to gratitude. Each day there is something new emerging in the world, brought there by the relationship I have with the Earth. A new leaf. A cluster of ladybird eggs. The first violets of spring. The blush of orange creeping across the pumpkin in autumn. What are you grateful for today?

GRATITUDE MEDITATION

Gratitude can be a part of your daily mindfulness practice. Like following your breath or tuning into present sensation, it can be done in just a moment. These little moments add up, shifting your overall perspective to one of presence and joy. Gratitude can also be the focus of a longer, more deliberate meditation. Here is one you can practise in your garden.

Find a place in your garden to sit comfortably. Take several breaths, following the air as it is pulled into your chest and released. Feel the pressure of your sitting bones on the ground or chair beneath you as the Earth pulls you towards her. Feel the sensation of air on your skin.

Open your eyes if they are closed, and let them rest gently on whatever is in front of you. What has that object brought you? Why is it in your life? Try not to get caught up in a story about this plant or garden structure, but let the reason and gift of this object simply arise in your mind. Is there a reason for gratitude for this item? Usually there is. Everything in my garden has a little bit of a story, from the plants to the mulch on the paths to the reclaimed boards of the raised beds. What are the stories of your garden? What connections have brought these items before you at this point in time and what gifts will they bring you?

Now gently shift your attention to something else nearby. Let its story arise, and send it gratitude. Stay present to your body, your breath and the now as you glance gently about your garden, sending out thankfulness.

Lastly, send your own self gratitude. Your body, heart and soul make this garden what it is. Notice how your energy has shifted simply by feeling gratitude.

Going with
the Flow

To plant a fruit tree, I first dig a hole three times the size of the root ball. In heavy clay soil, this takes a while. While I shove the sharp spade blade into the thick dirt, jump on the back of the spade and lift out piles of tannish soil, the tree waits nearby. Once the hole is deep enough, I drag out the hose and fill a foot or so of the hole with water. It slowly seeps in. The flow of water into clay soil is not something I can rush. Pouring on too much water in an attempt to speed things up just makes the pit fill more, or if I am watering on the surface of the soil, it just runs off, wasting water. So while my hole sucks up water, I tinker in other parts of the garden, tasting peas and turning the compost.

Once the water is mostly absorbed, I pile a little compost into the bottom of my hole to hold up the root ball. I don't want to put too rich a compost in the pit, for the tree will have a rude awakening when it absorbs all these nutrients and then has to force its way into that dense clay layer below and around it. But a little will give it a boost, like giving your child a vitamin pill.

I unwrap the tree's root ball and hoist it into my hole, then fill the moat around the ball with another round of hose water. The root ball absorbs some water and the

clay hole slowly sucks up the rest. I trim branches off
bushes, munch more peas and scoop chicken poo out
of the coop. When the moat has disappeared, I fill the
area around the baby tree's roots with the clay I pulled
out of the hole, loosening clods as I go. I create a sort
of trench around the base of the tree to hold water.
I fill the trench, and let it soak in.

THE WAY THINGS ARE

I cannot rush how clay absorbs water; it flows in its own
time, on its own rules of relationship with soil. I cannot
make the apple tree grow ten feet and sprout fresh apples
in a day, or even a year. In the garden we work with
natural rules, things we cannot rush or control. Perhaps
this is why it helps us slow down our minds, entering
a state of our own flow. We develop an energized focus
as our attention is pulled away from the chatter of daily
life and into a relationship with our bodies and the land.
We settle into a state of enjoying what we're doing, even
if that is as simple as waiting for water to sink into soil.

I become aware, too, of how my own body is, just as it is. I may be frustrated that I cannot do something, but the limitation is no different from how fast water flows into roots. That's just the way things are right now. I become aware of my limitations, but also of my strength, for while I cannot lift rocks indefinitely without hurting my back, I am blessed with quite a bit of strength and ability. When I enter into the present moment of the garden – the tree alive and growing on its own terms, the water flowing into soil only as fast as the soil can accept it – I enter into what gifts I have to work with in this moment, no more and no less.

GIFTS FROM THE GARDEN

In fact, the garden gives us a little more to work with than we might have otherwise. The bacteria *Mycobacterium vaccae* in soil have been found to activate a group of neurons that produce the brain chemical serotonin, which helps us feel good. Healthy soil is literally an antidepressant. So perhaps as I prepared the earth to receive a baby tree, the soil effectively reached out to me, inviting me into further relationship. Meanwhile, the sun beamed ultraviolet B rays onto my skin, transforming cholesterol into vitamin D3, enabling me to use calcium effectively, strengthening my bones. Strong bones are a good thing in a gardener.

Gardening is a web, a patchwork, an ecosystem. You, the gardener, are at the centre, dancing or flowing with it all, in this moment, just as it is.

A Sense of
Community

In a community of gardeners, each of us has something to bring to the group. Our unique backgrounds, our families, where we are in life and what we are passionate about – all are like ingredients for stone soup. In the story of Stone Soup, a clever fellow asks the members of a community to each contribute to his soup, which so far consists only of water and a stone. Each person brings one item – a carrot, a potato, some salt. In the end everyone gets a bowl of soup and some new friends.

Sometimes gardeners can be more like the stone, sitting alone, doing our own thing. But even for those of us who are natural introverts, connecting with other like-minded gardeners strengthens our gardens and our own lives.

A COMMUNITY IS BORN

In Buddhism, a community is called a sangha. The spiritual sangha is based on the qualities of awareness, acceptance, understanding, harmony and love. An ideal gardening community would also include these qualities. As gardeners, we come from many different backgrounds, spiritual paths and gardening approaches, but we can all come together in a love of green and growing things. Community members can share the joy and pride of growing food or flowers. We can get excited about new techniques and resources. We can support each other when things don't go well. I find that my human gardening community is supportive on many levels, not just in the garden. When a member is struggling, or endures the loss of a loved one, we are there to support that person. When they want to celebrate, we are all there with a healthy dish to cheer them on. Love of the Earth and of each other are the foundations of our connection. Plants are powerful community builders, as we all rely on plants each day.

I didn't always have a human gardening community. My community actually grew out of a desire to legalize keeping chickens in an urban environment. We ended up bringing the largest group of citizens ever to an Aurora City Council meeting in support of legalizing urban chickens, and subsequently many of those people bonded through the experience. We connected online to talk about chickens, gardening and urban homesteading. Out of that group grew at least one small business selling organic feed, straw and honey, and one fledgling non-profit group supporting local refugees. Local coffee shops have become gathering places for knitting circles, and a local urban farm offers classes in beekeeping, gardening and more. While I have chatted over the fence with neighbours on all sides of me, and with people I meet at the farmers' market or feed store, in my case community came about through social media. But it all started because of three women meeting in the kitchen of a local city council representative who supports green living.

MEETING IN THE ETHER AND IN REAL SPACE

We live in an exciting time. Connections online enable people who might not otherwise connect to find each other. I believe connecting with people from all walks of life and all parts of the globe is bringing us into a new way of life on Earth, one of connection, compassion and awareness. While certainly much of what happens online is not so positive, for the most part a growing community only strengthens our interconnections.

My favourite aspect of these communities is when we meet in real space. A gardening friend let me know she had alpaca manure should I want some. She brought me four bags of the stuff, which I gleefully spread all over my garden beds. I gave her my branch clippings, which she will use to make a hugelkultur bed (a raised bed filled with rotting wood). Each spring we gather at a friend's house for a seed swap; I've acquired seeds from this that I wouldn't otherwise be able to obtain, and encouraged new gardeners while sharing my own saved seeds.

Whether you gather together online, in person or both, connecting with other gardeners strengthens not just your garden and theirs, but our whole world. I have an image of pockets of gardeners, chicken owners, beekeepers and general plant lovers, overlapping circles connected all over the Earth. These overlapping spheres bring the values of love, awareness, harmony and acceptance to wherever they are needed. Even when we begin with just a stone, we can make a nourishing dish to nurture the land and each other. We can cover the Earth with connection and compassion, and with green and growing things to heal the planet and our place on it.

The Joy of
Compost

Where I live, east of the Rocky Mountains at the beginning of the American Great Plains, my soil is solid alluvial clay. It speaks of the southern edge of glaciers, and before that, of an inland sea. Now rivers snake their way across the hard-packed soil, telling the tale of farmers who came to the new city of Denver when gold and coal called the masses. The alluvial clay can be hard to grow plants in. One of the gifts that makes gardening here at all possible is the miracle of compost. It never fails to delight me that one takes kitchen scraps, chicken droppings, dryer lint and hair from the hairbrush, mix it all together and get perfect soil. In climates with fluffy dark soil to begin with, compost is a convenient way to reuse what would fill up the rubbish bin, reducing your carbon footprint and transforming life's flotsam into wealth. Compost is an allegory of all of life: transforming waste into gold, with each little creature playing its part.

DOING WHAT NATURE DOES NATURALLY

I wonder why we call it something different from soil, for that is what compost is. The word comes from Old French and Latin for 'something put together', which speaks of the process of making compost. But really we are just doing what nature does naturally. In a forest with enough moisture and an abundance of soil microbes, compost just happens. Healthy soil and compost are no different, though compost is richer in organic material than most soil found in your garden. Perhaps we differentiate one from the other not just because we humans mechanically pile up waste products for microbes to do their thing, but also because those

96

things we toss in the pile aren't all from one ecosystem. My pile has eggshells from my own chickens, but also from store-bought eggs that come from all over. It contains banana peel and avocado skins as well as vegetal waste that might actually grow here naturally, such as raked-up grasses. Like us humans, my compost is a mush of cultures and nutrients. It is yet another example of the power of diversity.

A MATTER OF DEATH AND LIFE

Without soil microbes turning death into life, life as we know it could not exist on Earth. One gram of garden soil can hold up to a billion bacteria. As compost moves through its stages of transformation, the varieties of bacteria and fungi change. The first wave of creatures breaks down the soluble components of soil, producing heat in the process. This is what warms a heap. This first community is replaced by heat-loving microorganisms, which break down fats, protein and cellulose. When they have transformed what they can, the heap cools again and the first wave of bacteria returns. Compost is a dance. It is a waxing and waning of energetic transformation, a rising and falling of life and death. It is a process where each tiny being has a purpose, just as does every other being on Earth. We can be reminded that to everything there is a season, and for every process there is a gift.

When the heap looks like garden soil from a magazine (or as close as we can get it), we spread it around the base of our plants. It is fertilizer, mulch and soil all in one. The pH of compost hovers perfectly in the middle, not too acidic or alkaline, so it helps to balance garden soil. It is a perfect metaphor for balance, a sort of Goldilocks Amendment.

CREATING LIFE COMPOST

The release of nutrients from compost happens slowly over time, a gentle nursing of the plant's roots. Because it's been broken down in multiple processes, compost is light and fluffy, creating space for water and air.

Compost continues transforming, inviting more life to flourish in the form of further bacteria, fungi, worms and insects. Compost is that sweet spot of nourishment that all life longs for. It is a reminder that all is provided in time, that nature wants to nurture, and we can be a part of this process in the garden. Perhaps we can develop metaphorical compost in other areas of our lives, drawing on the lessons of compost to make our lives richer. Mix the odds and ends of advice from friends with events from the past and snippets of inspiring articles, aerate with a deep cleansing breath, churn the mix in the pile of dreams and in time you will have fluffy, light nourishment to keep you going. Life compost.

The Scent
of the Garden

Can you conjure up a scent memory of
fresh rosemary leaves? Wet soil after a
shower of rain? The first violet of spring?
What are your scent associations with the
garden? Smell ties us to place and experience as much
as images and sounds; for some, smell might create
even stronger associations and memories. Smell is the
only fully developed sense at birth. Smell molecules
go straight to the brain, accessing memory and stress
centres directly. When we talk about scent, we often
think of essential oils or other strong smells. But even
subtle scents in the garden are part of what make us
slow down and connect with the Earth.

A friend of mine who lived in Hawaii for several years breathes deeply when we visit the tropical greenhouse in the local botanic gardens. The smell 'is Hawaii' for her. In this same greenhouse, there is a little terrarium housing poison dart frogs. Through the mesh on the top you can smell the mosses, flowing water, plants and humusy soil. There is a dankness but also sweetness. It smells like life. The scents in both indoor and outdoor gardens can bring us straight to emotional centres of the brain that speak to something ancient and wordless. Scent helps us understand the land.

SNIFFING OUT INFORMATION

Plants communicate through scent. The smell of freshly cut grass is a call for help. Flowers make scents that call to their specific pollinators, some sweet as vanilla (literally) and some distasteful (to us) as rotten flesh. I wonder if we humans could cultivate the ability to read plant scents, to know what weather is coming or what minerals are missing from the soil through the scent of a plant's leaves and flowers. I wouldn't be in the least surprised to discover that this is a latent skill we once had as hunter-gatherers. The best-smelling plant might lead us to the most nutritious seeds, for instance. One would be like a plant whisperer, but a plant smeller instead.

Farmers historically used scent (and also taste) to determine the make-up and health of soil. We can still tell if soil contains lots of clay or organic material from its scent. The former smells dusty and damp, while the latter is sweeter and might smell mossy or like leaf litter, sort of like the frog terrarium at the botanic gardens. Soil that has too much ammonia or that smells rotten or swampy might indicate the need for aeration and added compost. We can add that to the list of mindful gardening tasks: besides plant smellers, we need soil smellers. Perhaps it's not a full-time job, but taking time to smell your soil, your plants and the compost in your garden will likely tell you something you don't have to search for online to understand. The scents speak to a primal relationship with the land.

THE SCENT OF MEMORIES

Smells, like colours, are hard to describe, but we often know just what a person is talking about, having experienced that distinct smell ourselves. One scent that always stirs the senses even has a name, coined by two Australian scientists in the 1960s: *petrichor*, from petro (relating to rocks) and ichor (the fluid that flows in the veins of the gods). It's the scent of rain hitting parched soils and dry tarmac. Just the memory of this smell takes me back to summer in the Pacific Northwest – fat raindrops hitting the supermarket car park to clean and cool the hot summer air, and the metallic, dusty scent of petrichor. I remember not only the images, but the feeling. To me, petrichor smells exciting, full of possibility, but also safe and comfortable.

Scent is an important part of sensory gardens for people with visual impairment or other limitations. We can all enjoy sensory gardens, however, running our hands over the soft and pungent woolly thyme, inhaling the scent of chocolate cosmos and sniffing the pineapple mint. Scent is a way, therefore, that we can make our gardens more inclusive and compassionate. Include in your scent garden smells that take you back to a cherished garden memory, like your grandmother's roses, or lavender for that trip to Provence. My friend who missed Hawaii might grow spicy-scented *Matthiola incana*, or stock flowers. I could include a stone birdbath that invites the scent of petrichor. What would you include in your sensory memory garden? All you need then is a meditation cushion or a bench, and you've created a healing garden of your own. The scent garden can be a place to know yourself better, a place to invite trusted friends and share with them your stories, and invite them to share their own.

Coping
with Frustration

Where I live, the month of August is hot and dry. The bounty of spring spinach and peas has long been consumed and replaced. The final harvest of pumpkins and the larger tomatoes has yet to come. Beneath the scorching sun, my plants begin to wither. Hardier weeds creep in. Fruit doesn't set. Discouragement grows.

Many things can kill a garden. Hail. Heat. A scourge of locusts. As the garden's attendant, we can feel like we are a failure when the garden doesn't do well. Especially when our friends post photos on social media of an Eden-like paradise and all we have to show is a bug-infested mass of flowerless vines.

A bug's social media is the wind, on which she sends a chemical message to others of her kind saying, 'Good eats here!' Then more come to play and chomp and make our garden look a right mess. But she is happy, as are her offspring.

Should we gardeners be happy for the bug? Maybe. My loss of a tomato is more disappointment than true hardship. For many people, the loss of a crop equals true suffering and death. So perhaps I can take the loss of a crop as a moment to pause in gratitude for the fact that I will still eat tonight, as will my children.

And yet the frustration is real. To squash down my own sorrow when all my courgettes rot from the inside and I don't know why does no one any good, least of all me. So when my garden does poorly, I have to hold the dialectic of grief and acceptance. I am sad, even angry. The compost benefits when I toss a whole crop of 'useless' courgette plants in the heap. My perspective is valid, and so too is the perspective of the bugs and the nematodes that benefit from the loss of my garden.

In mindfulness, we can hold both. We can hold, too, the tension of holding both perspectives. We breathe into that space.

WE ARE ONE AND WE ARE TWO

A garden is a relationship, or many intertwined relationships. In any relationship, there is connection and there is separateness. That is the (somewhat confusing) dynamic of every relationship: we are one and we are two. Always. We are of the world and we are separate from the world. When I hug my partner, I am connected to him, and at the places where we touch, we are also aware of our being separate. Our boundaries, where I end and he begins are also where we connect.

When all is going well in the garden, I am not as aware of this ever-present dialectic, how I am part of my garden and at the same time wholly distinct from it. When the garden starts to fail, I see more clearly how my desires – a bounty of vegetables and a flourish of flowers – are maybe not the desires of the insects or the chickens who consumed my crop. I become uncomfortably aware of how I am not actually in charge here. When the cause of my garden's 'failure' is even further out from my usual awareness, like a hailstorm or a late frost, I am forced into awareness of all the greater relationships I am in. I am a part of the planet and its weather, and yet I am my own self, distinct from my surroundings. Ebb and flow.

THE BIGGER PICTURE

So when my garden fails, I become aware of energies greater than me, which can be overwhelming and confusing, but this awareness can also help me to see that perhaps failure is not what it seems. There is the story of the farmer whose horses ran away, and the village said, 'Oh, too bad'. Then the horses came home and brought some wild horses with them. The villagers said, 'Oh, how lucky!' Then his son was training the wild horses and was thrown and broke his leg. 'Oh, too bad', the villagers said. But then the army came looking for soldiers to recruit, and did not enlist the boy with the broken leg, and the villagers said, 'Oh, what luck!', for the boy's life would be spared. There is a bigger picture, and when the garden fails, we can keep in mind this larger picture, even when we don't know exactly what that is. We can give it up to the cosmic compost and move on.

Listen to the
Falling Rain

Without water in some form, we cannot garden. Wells and moisture stored in the soil through permaculture techniques are very useful, but what a garden needs, at least to some degree, is rain. Rain brings not only non-chlorinated water, but each drop also contains a particle of soil. Rain clouds and storms carry soil around the Earth, sharing minerals with gardens downstream. Rain connects us with everyone else on Earth.

TOO LITTLE, TOO MUCH . . .

A few years ago, we experienced a pretty severe drought. Though I watered from the hose and by using grey water from our showers, my plants didn't do very well.

They grew stunted and didn't produce fruit. The water that comes from my tap wasn't sufficient to nourish my plants; the chlorine and other chemicals were perhaps obstacles the plants had to overcome. My garden needed the natural, unaltered gift of real water. Rain brings life.

Too much rain, though, is of course just as problematic. One summer we experienced a ninety-day stretch of measurable precipitation, and while our tomato plants were massive and dark green, they produced no fruit. More rain than that, or lots of rain in a short time span, and we experience flooding. No gardens – save rice paddies – can recover from severe floods. So rain teaches us about the nourishing gifts of nature, but also about balance and gratitude. We hope for just the right amount of rain, and when it comes we are filled with a sense of things being right in the world.

Before plumbing, rain and various aqueduct systems were all we had to water our fields. Drought meant death, and even the end of whole civilizations. In parts of Africa and Asia, this is still true. It is no wonder that across many cultures we find rain gods or guardians, like Dudumitsa from Bulgaria, the Yoruban Oya and Aztec Tlaloc. Rain, both literal and metaphorical, is mentioned throughout the Bible. Rain is life. We are learning, too, that even in industrialized, developed nations, we cannot just do whatever we like with rain and the rest of the planet's water. Draining aquifers faster than they can replenish, we are upsetting the balance of the planet's life-giving water. Perhaps we need to return in some way to water management practices based on mindful gratitude.

FIFTY WORDS FOR RAIN

Rainstorms come in many different flavours. Perhaps we gardeners could come up with fifty descriptive nouns for rain. There is light, misty rain like one finds in a cloud forest. Pounding rain that strips leaves off the trees. A gentle rain you know will last all day, or even for several days (my favourite). Rain can come in bursts, just enough to wet the pavement and fill the air with petrichor, then blow past. Summer rain clears the air and makes fat droplets in the dust. When I worked at a plant nursery one summer, a heavy rain falling on the corrugated roof brought a halt to all conversation. Moss-creating rain is somewhere between mist and gentle rain. Early winter rain sinks into your bones and urges you to curl up with a gardening book instead of going outside. What kind of rain do you love?

AN INVITATION FOR MINDFULNESS

Often when it rains, I feel calmer and more settled. Partly this is because of low pressure; I could always get my sensitive toddler to nap in the afternoons when a storm came through. Also, I feel calmer because while life doesn't stop for rain, we get a sort of reprieve from going and doing so much when wet stuff is falling from the sky. But also I think rain reflects the soul of an introvert, yin and quiet. As sky and Earth are united through water, we come gently into ourselves. Rain is an invitation for mindfulness.

Listening to rain can be a simple meditation. Next time it rains, take time to become present through the sound of the rain. Hear it patter on the window or pound on the roof. Let your breath move in and out of your lungs. Can you feel more moisture in the air? You are breathing in water from some other place on Earth. You are here now, in this intersection of time and space, weather and breath. Close your eyes and let the sound become you. Water is life. You are life. All is one.

A Symbol of
Hope

When I weaned my son, I had been pregnant or
nursing my children for seven years. I was exhausted,
and the hormonal shift in my body set off a cascade of
events that led to severe adrenal fatigue. I experienced
panic attacks, hypoglycaemia, dizzy spells and terrible
insomnia. These had been building for years, but I could
no longer ignore the messages my body was giving
me. It was time to slow down, take care of myself and
heal. This even included not doing much in my garden,
as I didn't have the energy to dig and haul and chop.
Gardening keeps me going, though, so while I let many
things go that spring, I did what I was able. My garden
became one of my tools for healing.

One of the additions to my garden that spring was a pair of young pear trees. I mail-ordered them, and found a spot in the front garden. I took a few days instead of an hour to dig the holes, returning to my bed to rest afterwards. When the baby trees arrived, it was a windy day that threatened a hailstorm. At a mile elevation, thunderstorms are not to be taken lightly, but I needed to plant these trees. My mental health depended on it. So as wind whipped around me and thunder rolled closer and closer, I tucked these five-foot-tall, bare-root trees into the earth. I watered them, filled their holes with soil and said a prayer. I wasn't really sure they would make it, as many young bare-root trees have perished in my garden; the clay is hard to penetrate, hard to extract nutrients from. I wasn't sure I would make it, either, for severe adrenal fatigue can take years to repair and can even be fatal. The thunder boomed in response to my prayer of hope. But the trees did survive, and so did I. They haven't yet fruited; perhaps my own fruit is still ripening too, as

I figure out what my own calling in life looks like – an ever-evolving process. What keeps us going as we find our own paths is hope; those pear trees give me hope.

LIFE GOES ON

Every garden is a prayer, a promise of hope. We don't know what will hinder our garden's growth. Hailstorms, drought, insects. Maybe life will call us away and the flowers will die of neglect. Maybe a neighbour's dog will dig up our carefully tended plants. We cannot know for sure that plants will grow, mature, be harvested. But we plant anyway. We water, pluck off pests, stake trees and pile on more compost. We hope.

Perhaps this is why memorial gardens are so fitting. When we lose someone, we want to remember them through hope and life. In Denver, the Troy Chavez Memorial Peace Garden honours the lives of young victims of gang violence. The garden includes murals painted by local artists and a statue of Quetzalkóatl, an Aztec spirit who taught people to be kind and to remember that 'there is something or someone greater than ourselves'. When a garden bursts back into life year after year, green and vibrant, alive after the darkness of winter, we know that life continues despite our fears and pain.

TO HOPE OR NOT TO HOPE?

A seed is the epitome of hope. Inside its hard shell, a radicle hopes to become a root. The epicotyl hopes it will gain enough nutrients to grow into leaves. Once a seed germinates, the plant hopes for the right conditions to grow fruit and then more seeds, that life may continue. I think of the parents who created the Troy Chavez Memorial Peace Garden, and I imagine the little seeds of hope they held in their own hearts that speaking up and digging in, while it could not bring back their sons, could offer healing and hope to others.

I had a science teacher in college who hated hope. He argued that when we 'hope' something will come about, we give up a sense of internal responsibility.

We place the energy necessary for change in something outside of us, whether we hope that someone else will make something happen or that a higher power will magically induce change. He didn't believe in a higher power at all, again arguing that the only power that gets things done is our own. To me, however, hope pulls us forward. In the midst of the temptation to give up, that seed of something outside me that will help me continue, whether that be a simple garden seed, a pear tree or a whole garden, gives me the strength I need to keep going. I don't simply hope that the garden will flourish and then give up my own power, I grasp on to the hope that the garden provides me, and commit to the change and the growth that needs to happen.

Bees:
Essence of a Garden

Second only to the sight of a germinating seedling bursting from the soil, the hum of a bee invokes in the gardener a joyful sense of delight. Her fuzzy, pollen-covered rear end waggling inside a blossom promises that life will go on. Her determination to collect a flower's nectar and gather a basket of pollen reflects our own dedication to the cultivation of plant life, and we feel for her a deep sense of gratitude. Her buzzy hum invites us to pause in our own busyness, straighten up and stretch, as we watch her flit from flower to flower.

Have you ever sat beneath a crab apple tree in spring, its flowers literally humming with bees? While of course we know that the hum comes from the thousands of bees vibrating their veil-like wings, the sound seems more like a chant, like a collection of monks singing to the sun and the tree and the flowers, offering sweetness in exchange for pollination. In sitting beneath such a bee tree there is an answering vibration from inside ourselves as our own energy entrains with the collective hum. An ancient chord sounds from within. Closing your eyes, you may see in your mind's eye the golden rays of the sun, the fuzzy yellow of a bumblebee and the amber of honey dropping from a spoon. In pausing to listen to the buzz of a bee, we return to the primal hum of home.

A CREATURE OF THE SUN

The bee is a creature not just of our home the Earth, but also of the sun. The honeybee's waggle dance to her sisters communicates the location of nectar sources using the sun as a reference point. We might participate in bee perception when planning the garden, for we too orient our garden beds and rows to the sun. We notice where the shadows fall in winter, and in summer where we have areas of complete sun or part shade. The garden and the bee remind us that all life comes from the sun. The bee depends on the sun to warm things up enough for her to fly; the plant depends on the sun to make food for itself, the bees and us; and we depend on the sun to make the garden possible. No matter our climate or growing zone, we gardeners – and bees – are united in our attention and connection to the sun.

THE BEE COMMUNITY

Usually when we think of bees, the honeybee comes to mind. One reason for the honeybee's success on Earth – they evolved from wasps hundreds of millions of years ago and haven't changed much since – is her social nature. Her hive is a superorganism, made up of thousands of individuals. The hive cannot exist without its members, and the individuals cannot survive without the hive. This is true of us humans, too. We depend on each other just as bees do, though we readily get

mired in our arguments of difference and forget our
interdependence. Bees and the garden can gently bring
us back into the reality of our interconnection and need
for community. When we share extra produce with
a neighbour or a food bank, attend a seed swap in the
spring or can tomatoes with a group, we cultivate
community that strengthens our bodies and souls.
We are all of the one great hive.

THE YIN AND YANG OF BEES

The bee, not unlike us humans, is a creature of
contradiction. She gently visits delicate flowers to
gather sweet nectar in order to transform it into
miraculous honey, yet she carries with her always the
power to inflict pain. She invites us, therefore, to hold
the dialectic of life and death, yin and yang. Nothing
is ever totally what it seems. Even bee venom, which
we usually think of as bad (bee stings are painful, and
even fatal to those prone to anaphylaxis), has the
potential to cure serious disease. Holding the dialectic

invites us into the present moment, out of our labels and judgements, in observation of the unfolding of life. We let go of trying to control, and simply watch the bee making her rounds from blossom to blossom in search of the goodness of life. We slow down, and we breathe.

No-dig
Gardening

We humans are good at making tools, discerning chemical properties and moving the earth to suit our needs. These skills are partly what make us human, and they have immense value. Sometimes, though, we need to learn to do less. To step back and allow nature to engage in the complex and dynamic processes she has perfected over millennia. In 'no-dig' or 'no-till' gardening, we have to step back and trust the flow. In this technique, you don't dig, turn over or till the garden soil before planting. Using a broadfork or pitchfork, you aerate the soil gently by pushing the tines into the soil. On top of the existing soil, pile on layers of compost, leaves and other materials. Then layer on an inch or three of compost, and plant seeds or seedlings in this top layer. In another version of this technique, called hugelkultur, logs or sticks are piled and covered with compost to break the wood down into fluffy soil.

Both of these approaches to creating a garden bed require in the gardener a great deal of trust in nature. In the case of hugelkultur, patience is also required, as it can take years for the wood to break down. Although you can plant on the hugelkultur pile the first season, if the chemistry isn't quite right, you get mixed results. I have tried several hugelkultur beds in various places about my garden, and I find it hard to just step back and let it do its thing. I want to speed things up. Yet when I change my mind about where a bed will go and pull out the half-rotted logs, the soil surrounding those logs is the fluffiest, compostiest soil in my garden. So I know it works, even short term. Now I just have to be patient enough to see it through. I need to be as patient growing soil as I am growing plants.

TAKING THE LONG VIEW

One of the best garden seasons I've experienced in my current house grew from a layered bed. In the autumn, we put cardboard down on the hard-packed, sun-baked dust that made up part of our garden. On top of this we piled grass clippings and leaves sprinkled with blood meal, then compost. It sat and cooked all winter, and in the spring I planted red Hopi corn, green and purple tomatillos, yellow pear tomatoes and more. It grew into a verdant jungle with enough tomatillos to share with our new neighbours, and countless green tomatoes for my infant daughter to chomp.

So now I add layers on top of each bed I build, only fluffing the clay layers beneath by poking a pitchfork into the soil and leaning back gently to aerate. I plant cover crops. With the new hugelkultur beds, I wait. I make my tinkering mind take a little holiday. Though I want to dig and turn and move things about, I know they have to stay put and cook. Soil development takes time, fungi, water, soil microbes and more time.

What helps my impatient, engineering mind to relax a little is to see the whole process over time spans. Perhaps right now my garden consists of soil and tomato plants, but in a few months the fruits of those plants will be eaten, turned into me and my family. The plants will be chopped up and thrown into the compost pile. Parts of the old soil will be consumed by the plants, transformed into leaves and fruits. In a few years' time, what has become of that plant, that soil? In another geological age, it will likely not look like a garden at all.

A STONE IN THE RIVER OF TIME

As a gardener, I am a stone in the river of time, causing it to swirl around me instead of just flow on by. As fungi transform wood into soil, nematodes transform soil into nutrients, nutrients turn seeds into greenery, sunlight changes greenery into fruit, I am but one spot on the river of transformation, requesting through the process a garden. Then I don't need to tinker impatiently, but only dance with the flow over time.

No-dig gardening trusts the flow, but also makes gardening easier for us. We nourish the soil instead of forcing it to do our will. We slow down and listen to the ancient processes alive in the soil. We realize the soil is in fact alive, and to bring more living energy to our own lives, we need to support this dynamic living process. When we become a part of the long-term process of life, our own lives, and our gardens, are utterly transformed.

Permaculture

Several movements in the gardening world address
the fact that the garden is a dynamic and complex
set of relationships flowing over time; permaculture,
or 'permanent agriculture' is one of these holistic
approaches to gardening. Permaculture focuses on
perennial food production, low impact on the Earth,
sharing our bounty and mimicking nature. The approach
acknowledges that we are a part of nature, and that to
solve the problems caused by industrialization, we have
to think holistically. Humans and our needs can be a
part of solutions, not just a series of problems at odds
with nature. In fact we are co-creators with the plants,
cultivating life together.

THE PLANT GUILD

One of the central ideas in permaculture is the plant guild. In the non-gardening world, a guild is a group of artisans working to support each other; in the permaculture guild, a central plant (usually a food-bearing tree) forms the foundation of a group of interconnected plants. Around the base of the tree grow plants of differing heights and purposes, creating a miniature ecosystem that supports long-term food production.

This simple design concept reflects many of the ideas of mindful gardening. First, we see the dynamic ecosystem, and how a collection of plants is more than the sum of its parts. Even if you only grow a single rosemary plant in your kitchen window, you have encountered how gardening is more than just growing plants: a new relationship with the world forms as you relate to this plant, it relates to the soil and so on. The more plants we grow, the more complex these relationships become. In gardening, as in the world, diversity is strength. The plant guild builds on this idea deliberately.

Second, the plant guild centres around a long-term food source, which often produces far more food than one person or even a family can eat. If you have ever grown a fruit tree, you know the bounty it provides, a bounty you share with others. When I was young, my uncle had two apple trees on his small suburban property. Every autumn we had an apple-picking party, where the uncles would get together to drink a lot and pick apples. One uncle would climb the tree and shake it to get as many apples down as possible. I still recall the thunking noise of dozens of apples hitting the ground. Apple trees came to represent family, community and autumn parties with cider. A fruit tree is not just a tree, but a community of insects, a home for birds and a food producer that brings people together. It is the centre of the permaculture plant guild in part because it is taller than the surrounding plants, but also because a fruit tree is the centre of the garden and the community. It is the proverbial provider of sweet nourishment and connection with nature.

Beyond the tree, we find further relationships – soil, earthworms, fungi, nematodes – plus more we may never even know about. When I begin to picture this world of plants and creatures and soil, I come up against my own not knowing. I feel awe. I want to sit at the base of the apple tree and take it all in. Any tree can become the Bodhi tree, under which Siddhartha Gautama – the Buddha – gained enlightenment.

FROM A PROBLEM, AN OPPORTUNITY

Another concept in permaculture that can inform our study of mindful gardening practices is that of regarding problems as opportunities. For instance, if your garden is overrun by slugs, a permaculturist sees this as an opportunity to bring in ducks, who will eat the slugs, fertilize the garden and provide eggs. In my own garden, I have way too much bindweed and other weeds I cannot just ask to move out. Weeds become food, soil remediation and future compost. When they get too big or start to take over cultivated plants, I pull them up and stuff them in a black plastic bag to cook the weed seeds, then I add the weeds to the compost. From a problem, an opportunity. It takes a mindful approach to gardening – and life – to see these opportunities and design solutions. I have to slow down, take a few breaths and listen to what the land is telling me. From listening and observing, plus looking for the opportunity in my interconnected network of dynamic relationships, grow new pathways and discoveries.

Permaculture and mindful gardening are both about recognizing and participating in the big picture. We are part of a whole, bigger than we can ever really know. A plant guild, perennial food crops and turning challenge into opportunity each help us see and understand this big picture. Then we just need to take a moment to sit by the tree of awareness and breathe.

The
Harvest

Most countries or cultures hold a festival
to celebrate the harvest, and some have
several for individual crops. In the Celtic
spiritual calendar, there are three harvest
festivals. In the Northern Hemisphere,
there's one in August, another in
September and the final one in October;
in the Southern Hemisphere they fall
in February, March and April. The first is
Lammas – the mass of the loaf – and while
it is usually celebrated on 2 August in the north,
it can also be celebrated when berries are ripe. I like this
marker, as it follows the Earth's rhythms more closely.

Where I live, summer is still in full swing in August; yet there is a subtle shift in the air. I can feel the edge of autumn. And if I'm lucky, I'll get a few berries from the garden. Growing up, late summer was all about berries. I lived in a place where blackberries grow thick and wild. We picked as many as we could – ideally, enough to pack the freezer full of succulent dark purple berries to last almost till spring.

I appreciate the berry harvest because it reminds us that metaphorical harvests can come in waves, not just one big yield of insight or return. Wheat, berries, corn, squash and cabbages – the harvest is a parade lasting many months. I find personal insight to be the same. I realize something, integrate it, reveal something more, contemplate that, then harvest further insight later on. Often I don't know what I'm harvesting personally until long after the event. Just as we cannot harvest a fruit before it is ripe, we will not understand the messages of personal growth until these insights are themselves ripe, or until we are ready to receive the harvest.

SURPRISE HARVEST

Have you ever discovered something coming up in the garden and you have no memory of planting it there? Or perhaps you have grown squash plants and when the fruit forms it looks nothing like the variety you thought you were getting. We can approach this surprise mindfully by accepting what is and being open and curious. Maybe the mystery plant will be just what you wanted, or maybe it will turn out to be an invasive weed. The squash might be a fabulous hybrid, or it might be best fed to the chickens. Either way is fine. It just is.

We can bring the same openness to our internal harvest. We don't always know where self-discovery and personal growth will lead. Often when we're trying to heal a past trauma or develop a new part of ourselves, we can be a bit demanding. We expect ourselves to grow faster, be better, be more. From a Buddhist perspective, we become attached to our ideal self, believing it to be more real than what actually is true. In reality, we are all a mix of mystery vegetables and prizewinners, and it's all okay. Mindfulness shows us that what is now is all that is actually real. And even that is illusion. We don't know what is real. All we can do is be present to what is, noticing our breath, our 'self', the strange butternut-spaghetti-pumpkin squash. The garden teaches us we cannot hurry the ripening. We can only sit and allow things to unfold, meeting them where we are with the watering can.

Then out of that noticing, a harvest. It just arises. We might have to water it a little, tuck a little compost around it, but we don't have to effort the squash into being. It is there. Slowly growing, and then we can pick it and see what we have. Self-fruition is the same. We are responsible for taking care of ourselves by eating right, getting enough quality sleep, expressing our feelings in ways that honour ourselves and others, and then, our true self arises. It is our spiritual nature, when we are aligned with care and balance, to bloom into our higher selves, one step at a time.

GATHERING IN AND LETTING GO

The harvest time, whether berries or pumpkins or inner growth, is a time of gathering riches, but it is also a time of letting go. In order to harvest something, part of it has to die. Most harvest festivals honour this double-edged sword, life and death as one continuous dance. When we go through personal growth, the same is true. As we rejoice in our new discoveries, we need also to give ourselves time to grieve and let go. And then, when we have fully released our old selves, we can crack open the fruit before us and discover what lies inside: seeds for the future. This is the nature of the harvest: a release of the past, a gift in the present and a promise of hope for the future.

Cool-season
Garden

Perhaps you share with me the need to garden.
Where I live, this means I feel bereft and aimless from
November to March, when I can't plant anything in
the ground and the harvest is minimal. One way I have
remediated this loss is to plant cool-season crops under
a simple low hoop of plastic in early autumn, so that I
get greens in winter. I'm not always successful at getting
the timing right, as the heat of early autumn can be too
high to germinate cool-season seeds like spinach, and
when they do germinate they can fry under the plastic
covering. But when I get it right, there is nothing like
the triumphant gratitude of picking a bowl of salad
greens while the world is frozen.

The greens from a hoop house or cold frame are unlike any you will buy at the store, and even different from spring garden greens. Winter veggies are tough. Their cell walls are strong against the cold, able to survive cycles of freezing and thawing. Their roots hold strong under the soil, protected just enough to stay alive. The leaves are dark green, and tend to be small and dense. They match the feeling inside me in winter: sturdy, rooted, biding time till spring.

The cool-season garden suggests, however, that while winter is a time of dormancy and rest, with a little shelter there can still be life and growth. Sometimes we can be like dandelions growing in cracks – nothing can hold us back; we are diamonds in the rough. But after a while, without support, we wither and stop growing. We need a kind soul to bring us a little water, a little encouragement. We are more like tender perennials than hardy dandelions. When our needs are heard and respected, when we are given just a little boost of natural fertilizer at the right time, we can flourish.

THE WINTER TUNNEL OF LIFE

At times, it feels like our own ground is frozen solid
and we can't garner enough nutrients to keep going.
I experienced this when my children were growing out
of their baby stage, and it was time for me to figure
out the next steps in my life. I was debating pursuing
a teaching licence, but I felt hesitant leaving behind
my work as an energy healer and massage therapist,
and moving on to something new. Yet I hadn't been
wholly happy as a healer. It felt like a pot that didn't
quite fit my root ball. Then, out of the blue, I was asked
to substitute teach for a day, and it was enough to
show me how much I love teaching. It is just the right
sized pot for me. I just needed that little nudge to
show me the way.

I'm mixing metaphors here, but whether we're
talking pot size to root ball or frozen ground beneath
a winter tunnel, what it all amounts to is that we need
the right ground to support us, the right climate to
keep us going. Gardening in any season reminds us

that the spark lives in us at all times, but we need that call, that request, that support to pull us where we need to go. Then, when the time is right, we can flourish.

One autumn I planted spinach beneath a plastic tunnel, and though it grew just tiny little leaves before the frost, it came back in very early spring. By April, when spinach can be planted in an unprotected bed, I had such a jungle of greens I was giving away bags to friends. With that little bit of protection, my spinach was able to flourish when light and temperatures began to increase. The same has been true for my work as a teacher. The process I went through to change careers mid-life, to find the best place for me to root, wasn't always easy, but it felt right. And when all the pieces were finally in place, I was like that spring crop of spinach, sharing my love and my gifts with others. Is anything waiting beneath your metaphoric winter tunnel, ready to burst into new life? How can you support this rebirth? There is always growth, always life, even in the dark and cold of winter.

When you do not know what is waiting to unfold and grow, the trick is to go into the silence of the winter tunnel. Listen to the stillness. Don't direct or label or force, just listen. In stillness and silence sometimes what we need to hear is revealed. Then we must let it germinate in its own time.

The Garden
Under Snow

Under a blanket of snow lies a curled emerald dragon, her breath slow but unceasing. She shimmers like a will-o'-the-wisp just outside your line of sight. We gardeners hear her voice in dreams, whispering promises of what the land will bring in a few months' time as she turns over in her hibernation. She is a pulse of life held in the belly of the Earth. We know she will wake in due time. For now, we watch her domain from inside the house, a mug of steaming tea in our grasp, waiting. We inhabit the realm of the North, of Earth energy and the mind. The garden under snow is the garden of thoughts and plans, dreams and ideas, stone and root. It beckons to us to slow down, settle in and breathe.

The winter garden is the garden of hoping for the best. It is a dream garden of huge plump tomatoes and bug-free broccoli, the one we have yet to plant but can nonetheless taste in our mind. It is the garden of plans: in winter we pore over seed catalogues, committing to try something new next spring. We mentally move carrots from one bed to another and wonder if perhaps violets might like that spot under the evergreens. We tap in to the dragon's dreams and ask her if there might be somewhere we could tuck another apple tree.

This winter garden of dreams and plans is no less real than the green and growing garden. A blueprint is no less real than a house. An engagement is as real – or more so – as the ring. When we run our fingers over the pages of a seed catalogue, marvelling at the greens and purples and oranges we have yet to grow, we plant seeds in our own mind, seeds of commitment and dreams. If you have ever had a dream and followed it through, you know how powerful these seeds of the mind and heart can be. This, too, is the garden.

CONTEMPLATING
THE GARDEN'S SKELETON

The winter garden covered in snow is a chance to appreciate the slower moving energies of a garden. We think that the flowers and fruits we get in warmer seasons equal the garden. But as I gaze out of my window at the snow-covered landscape, I see other energies, the garden of wood and stem, rock and earth. The snow-covered garden gifts us with the opportunity not just to dream and plan; we also see the land in a new light. With foliage gone and the ugly stillness of winter covered in soft curves of snow, we can see the garden's bones. This gives us a different perspective that can inform our dreaming. What do the stones and pathways, empty arbours and still birdbaths have to tell you? Can you see how energy flows through your garden and listen to the suggestions that a garden skeleton might offer? These perennial garden features are the container that holds the more active garden of green and growing things. In some cases, the stone and wood literally provide the container for our garden, and the fallow earth holds up both the garden and the gardener. The winter pathways and structure are an empty stage, ready to receive the actors and dancers of spring. This, too, is the garden.

More active than stone, but equally still in winter, are the roots of the perennial plants resting beneath the surface. In autumn, a plant pulls its sugars out of leaves and stem and into the roots. These underground vessels ensure the plant can rise again in spring, when water can once again flow. These, too, are the garden.

THE EVER-TURNING WHEEL

As we move around the wheel of time, through the seasons and all kinds of weather, we and the garden grow together. In winter, we can find this waiting, this stillness. Not unlike the still space we reach in mindfulness practice. Here we breathe, and witness as time unfolds. The wheel turns, and the mindful gardener knows to sit with whatever is right now, as well as to welcome dreams. We pack all these discoveries in the wheelbarrow, toting them down the paths of life. We come home to ourselves, as we grow in compassion and understanding. We see how our paths intersect with billions of plant and animal beings. We sit with the stillness and the promise, both, and know that in time the days of spring will come.

ACKNOWLEDGEMENTS

A heartfelt thank you to Tony, Sophie and Harper for helping me tend the Garden of Life. Thank you to my wonderfully supportive community for everything, from prayers to plants. May we fill the Earth with Love and Light, bringing Spirit to all we do.